Infertility

&

Adoption

A Story Of Divine Order

April Dawn Bridges

ISBN 978-0-9860143-6-9

All Scripture quotes are from the King James Bible.

Address All Inquiries To:
THE OLD PATHS PUBLICATIONS, Inc.
142 Gold Flume Way
Cleveland, Georgia, U.S.A.

"Thus saith the LORD, Stand ye in the ways, and see, and ask for the old paths, where is the good way, and walk therein, and ye shall find rest for your souls..." (Jeremiah 6:16)

Website: www.theoldpathspublications.com
Email: TOP@theoldpathspublications.com

1.0

DEDICATION

I would like to thank God for his love and mercy, for without this I would not be writing the words that fill these pages.

This book is dedicated to our two beautiful sons, Michael and Brett, without whom we would not have a story to tell. We love you both very much and thank God for you every day.

We extend a special thanks to our family and friends who have traveled this journey with us, giving their undying support. We also want to give particular thanks to our dear friends Corbett, Evelyn, Katrina, and also to our dear friend Wendy Lee. I could not have put this all together without you. I am so blessed to have had your love and support through this journey. May God bless you.

PREFACE

The Road of Infertility

The road of infertility is truly a hard road to travel. This book will not tell you how to conceive, nor will it inform you of any magic pills or potions. It will inspire you never to give up hope, for God does have a plan for our life, and this is *"Divine Order."*

Our Story

As you read this, you will walk through our story of infertility and just where that road took us. We are just one family, out of many, who have cried the tears and felt the pain of not being able to conceive. But, *"With God **all** things are possible."* (Matt.19:26) Through the telling of our story, we hope to remind you that you are not alone.

Our Account is Written to Our Boys

Our adoption stories are written to our boys with great love for them. Through reading their stories, you will find the love of God and how his plan for our lives became *"Divine Order."*

TABLE OF CONTENTS

CHAPTER 1

THE ROAD

"But as it is written, Eye hath not seen, nor ear heard, neither have entered into the heart of man, the things which God hath prepared for them that love him." (I Corinthians 2:9)

A Little Girl's Dream

When you were a little girl, as you played with your dolls, you pretended to be "Mommy" to all of them. If you were lucky, you would talk Johnny, who lived next door, into coming over and being the "Daddy;" that is, once you talked him out of his sandbox full of toys. If you were like me, as a little girl you always dreamed of getting married, having a house with a white picket fence, 2.1 kids, a cat and a dog. In other words, you dreamed of having a normal, happy life. For most little girls, that dream becomes a reality, but for others that dream will never be fulfilled.

My Childhood

As for me, having grown up in a solid

Christian home with a wonderful Mom and Dad, and a house full of brothers and sisters (six of us), I never thought for one minute that the idea of having children would only be a dream for me. I never even considered the possibility. I guess I just assumed I would have everything I dreamed of as a little girl.

Life's 'Ups and Downs'

Life does sometimes throw us curve balls, but just because they are curve balls doesn't mean that they are wrong or right...... only different. Sometimes the way we look at things in life isn't the same way God looks at things **for** our lives. Our time isn't always God's time. Patience is a virtue that we as humans struggle with.

"Knowing this, that the trying of your faith worketh patience." James 1:3

An Example

It's like getting up in the morning and running around, trying to get out the door as you run late for work, and everything is going wrong that could go wrong. You rush to get in your car, spill coffee on your shirt, then run back in and grab another one from the closet. It's not perfect but it will do. You get almost to work and the traffic has stopped completely and you are forced to take a detour from your normal route. Frustrated at the events of the morning, you pray for God's grace to get you through this day in one piece so that you may live to see tomorrow. Getting from point A to point B is not always a straight line.

God's Detours and Plans

Sometimes it takes that detour or curve ball to get us to what eventually we find to be the most beautiful place in our life. God's detours are his way of slowing us down and redirecting us to his greater plan...His *"Divine Order."* We can't always see what's ahead. Did you ever think that the coffee on your shirt or the traffic being stopped wasn't part of God's *Divine Order?* Maybe it was to keep you from being in the crash that was just ahead of you, or maybe it was to get you to slow down and take in your surroundings. God has a plan for all our lives; we just have to put ourselves aside and open ourselves to what God has in store for our lives. Believe me, I know that this is easier said than done. I've been there. But at least give it a shot... you may be surprised at what you find.

"Trust in the Lord with all thine heart; and lean not unto thine own understanding. In all thy ways acknowledge him, and he shall direct thy paths." Proverbs 3:5-6

A Little Walk Through Life

Ok, now let's go for a little walk.

You are all grown up now, no more playing with dolls and pretending. You are now a woman. I know that sometimes we all wish we could go back and be a little girl again, but guess what....we can't. If we did go back, we would have to do it all over again, all the heartache and pain, tears, silliness, adolescence, acne, boys and oh, so much more. Nope, I do not want to go back; so I will continue to move forward and continue to grow.

"Mister Right"

One day, you meet your "Mister Right," and you know that he is the **ONE.** As your relationship grows, you discuss marriage and children and decide that is what you both want. That's what I did. I married my "Mister Right." I married the love of my life; William. We both wanted children from the start but decided to wait at least a year so that we could settle down, save some money, and get into the whole married routine... whatever that means. Marriage does not come with an instruction book. It is a day by day learning curve and walk in faith.

A Miscarriage

For us, we had no problem getting pregnant once, but it ended in a miscarriage when I was about six to eight weeks along. We were devastated, heartbroken and in pain. Our faith was strong in that we knew God had a reason for this loss, but it still hurt. We would try again.

Failed Attempts at Getting Pregnant

Well into our second year of marriage we were still trying. Months passed and we knew in our hearts that something wasn't right. Why was it so hard to conceive again? Disappointment after disappointment time and time again... which really meant negative pregnancy test after negative pregnancy test. The frustration began to build and we decided it was time to go to the doctor for help. This is where all the medical testing and procedures began. It felt as if I were just one big number and aggravation in the medical world. The doctors, who were supposed to have all the answers, would just say to me "just give it a little more time, don't stress over it, it will happen, you're still so young," and the most famous words of all, **"you're trying too hard."** I hated those words with a passion.

The Frustrations

Sensing our frustrations, the doctors would draw blood each visit, just to make us happy, and then to make them happy they'd send me the bill. Does that sound familiar? I felt like I had given them enough blood to fill another human being! Then the test comes back.....and oh, the results. You want the results to be normal, but at the same time you wish they could find something that needed to be fixed. Well, my blood work always came back normal, normal, normal! I was ever-so-tired of hearing that word "normal!" I needed and wanted an answer as to why we were not conceiving a child, not just be told "everything is normal." Every time the doctor would say, "just keep trying" as he handed me a calendar and told me to keep track of my cycles. He also told me to buy a BBT (Basal Body Temperature) thermometer to tell me when I was ovulating so that we could schedule "marital relations."

Unexpectedly, something that was once thought of as a beautiful experience between husband and wife becomes work, work, work! Boy, did I come to hate that with a passion! At first it was fun and your man is very happy with this new arrangement, but after two, three, or perhaps four months, what once was passion in your marriage becomes a chore that no one is happy about....scheduled marital relations. Something about that just

18

isn't right, much less normal! Everything (and I do mean everything) is scheduled with a calendar and set by the watch that is laying beside your BBT chart. I hated it! This is not how it should be, so why Lord are you putting me through this?

Years three, four and five of our marriage came with new doctors, more tests and more procedures. The doctors thought if I had an HSG (Hysterosalpingogram), that would find the answer to all our prayers. Nope... all was clear with my tubes and no blockages were found. I was still asking, "why Lord?" What is in your bigger plan for William and me? I knew in my heart that God's timing was not for me, nor science, to question, and when it was right our prayers would be answered.

As for my dear sweet husband, oh, what this man was willing to go through. "Want a cup?" seemed to be the usual question. Well, he really didn't want one, but he was a real trooper and took it anyway. The SA (Semen Analysis) test showed a low sperm count and some malformations. The doctors told us that conception would be hard to achieve but not impossible, if we would "just keep trying." That small glimmer of hope, that there was finally an answer to our situation, vanished when sadness and disappointment walked right out of those doctors' doors with us every single time. As we left our appointments, and our hope for a family was crushed each and every time, sadness boiled out of my eyes and my heart. How much more beaten down could I/we get? William was my rock; always great, always supportive. He would look at me and say, "Honey, it will be okay. It will work out." He always carried a different outlook than I. It seemed as if he had a true sense of what God's plan would be for us, and that it would all be okay. I guess I couldn't see it at that moment.

> "Who is this King of Glory? The Lord strong and mighty, the Lord mighty in battle." Psalms 24:8

When you feel like dying, you should talk about living.

When you feel like giving up, you should talk about pressing forward.

When you don't see any way out, you should talk about how God can make a way.

And know this; the enemy always fights you the hardest when he knows God has something great in store.

Author Unknown

CHAPTER 2

THE ANGER

"My God, my God, why hast thou forsaken me? why art thou so far from helping me, and from the words of my roaring?

O my God, I cry in the daytime, but thou hearest not; and in the night season, and am not silent.

But thou art holy, O thou that inhabitest the praises of Israel.

Our fathers trusted in thee: they trusted and thou didst deliver them.

They cried unto thee, and were delivered: they trusted in thee, and were not confounded. Psalm 22: 1-5

A Dark and Lonely Place

I just wanted to die. What did all this mean? What were we supposed to do now? I prayed and he prayed, every day crying out to God for a child of our own. We had done everything humanly possible: blood work, procedures, infertility drugs and still no baby. I found myself in a place I never would

21

want anyone to be. This place was dark and lonely and I felt so abandoned by God.

I Was Angry With God

I was so angry with God. How could He do this to me? How could He do this to us? We were good people. We both loved God and were strong in our faith. We went to church, had a good solid marriage, nice home and were financially able to provide for a child....so, why God? Why? I couldn't understand. I cried myself to sleep night after night, month after month. I know that my dear husband was feeling like he had let me down as he saw my heart ache day after day. I never felt let down by William. I felt God had let us down.

My Heart Versus My Mind

My husband carried his anger well. I cried aloud. Sometimes I couldn't understand my faith, because even though I was so angry with God, I still prayed and still attended church. I still somehow, someway, knew that God must have something in mind for me. I just didn't understand what His will for me was. I carried the passage:

"And Jesus looking upon them saith, With men it is impossible, but not with God: for with God all things are possible." Mark 10:27

and read it daily. In my heart I truly believed this, but my mind was not so agreeable. If God truly loved me then why did He want me to have such heartache?

Lots of Anger, Shame, and Fear

I had anger and lots of it, along with shame and even fear. I had it stuck in my head that it was wrong and a sin to be angry at God, and that brought me to shame. Through those trying years I discovered that I was human; flesh and bone, and God is still all-knowing. I was and always will be a child of God. He is my friend through good times and bad.

Anger With My Best Friend

What would you do if you were angry, hurt, and confused with your best friend? Nine out of ten times you would go to your best friend and tell them that you were angry with them and you didn't like to feel that way toward them. You would have to talk it out, make amends and forgive.

My Best Friend

Well, I had come to that point in all my anger, that I had to do just that. I had to go to my best friend, get on my knees, and talk it over. I had to go to God, my best friend. I talked to God face-to-face, just as I would have talked to my earthly best friend. I cried and prayed. After I prayed and talked to God for a little while, I felt some peace. I say some peace, because I still had to heal, as we all do, after we have been hurt, broken and bruised.

Deep Spiritual Understanding

As the days passed, I still longed for a baby. I still hurt, but somehow I knew that God has to have a plan for my life; our life. Even though we had no idea what lay before us, we still had to keep the faith that God had an awesome plan that one day would be revealed to us when the time was right. "All things in God's time."

CHAPTER 3

A PART OF THE PLAN

Foster Parenting

In 1995, we were introduced to the idea of foster parenting. We decided that maybe, just maybe, this was what God's plan was for us. So we became foster parents for two children. This was truly a challenge. We were young, dumb and totally unprepared for what lay ahead of us.

Learning What True Love Is

Even though I came from a large family and thought I knew how to be a parent, I was clueless of how to be a "mom" to a 9-year-old little boy and a 3-year-old little girl. But I would certainly try to be the "mom figure" they needed. Here were two beautiful children entrusted to us, both with a lot of baggage, and I felt so helpless and like a failure. I was not prepared to understand nor handle what was facing me.

We had these two beautiful children in our lives for 15 very hard months. The "system" pushed and pushed for us to adopt them. We came very close to doing so, however struggling in our hearts to make the right decision for everyone involved. One night, after the children were asleep, I found myself lying in bed sobbing and crying aloud. I knew this situation was not right. This was not God's plan for us. I felt as if I were losing my mind! I was in a very dark place. At that moment, I knew what I had to do; what William and I had to do together. These two beautiful and precious children needed more than what we could give them. They needed someone who was older and wiser, who could give them what we could not. Oh dear God, please guide us; these children are depending on us.

> *"I can do all things through Christ which strengtheneth me."* Philippians 4:13

That night, William and I prayed with all our hearts and souls. We came to the decision that if we truly loved these children, we had to let them go. This was one of the most difficult and painful times in our lives that we had ever faced. Once again we were left with empty hearts and empty rooms. I questioned myself many times, wondering if we had done the right thing by letting the children go and stopping foster parenting altogether.

Leaving My Broken Heart at Jesus' Feet

I know in my heart that it was the right thing for all, but the pain was unbearable at times. I felt as if I had abandoned those children and abandoned my faith in God. I was mentally, physically and spiritually drained. I feared that my failure as a "foster mom" was God's way of saying that He would not fill our hearts and home with children ever again. I was breaking from the inside, and not just in my heart, and I felt I needed to pray and ask for forgiveness because I had failed. I fell on my knees and prayed out to God one more time, "God, please help me. I need you God. I feel, but I don't know what I feel. God, if you ever see fit to give me a child, I promise to not make the same mistakes that I have made in the past. I promise to give a child everything I have mentally, physically, spiritually and financially. God, I promise to give this child back to you. I will love this child with all my being until the day I die. God, if you see fit to bless us, I promise everything that I am and everything that you want me to be." I left my prayer and my broken heart at Jesus' feet that night.

The children left in November, 1996.

"But without faith it is impossible to please him: for he that cometh to God must believe that he is, and that he is a rewarder of them that diligently seek him." Hebrews 11:6

CHAPTER 4

A NEW DAY

"Now faith is the substance of things hoped for, the evidence of things not seen." Hebrews 11:1

Mother's Day, May 11, 1997

Wow! Where do I even begin to tell this part of the story? We were providentially told of a pregnant woman that chose life and wanted to give her baby up for adoption. Little did we know that her decision would eventually come to be our first-born child. We had no idea at this point how the events would unfold or even if this were actually part of God's plan for us. I had been praying for, and asking for, peace, from my best friend, God. God heard my cries and truly was giving William and me a clear sign of peace and forgiveness. But this journey was only beginning....

"It is past experiences and pain that make us whom we are today, and it is past pain that makes us the parents we are now."

A True Hero

It was the Monday after Mother's Day, May 12, 1997, that I spoke to a true hero; a woman that chose the life course for her unborn child. She was 5 months pregnant and wanted to give the baby up for adoption so that he or she could have more in life than she could offer. We spoke for the longest time, as if we had always known each other. Her words were kind and sincere. I could not wait to meet her face-to-face.

Astonishment

I told William about my conversation with this woman. He told me that this was the craziest, most hare-brained idea I had ever had and that no one in her right mind would just give her baby away. I told him I knew that it sounded crazy, but I really had a good feeling about this. I'm sure by this point, this wonderful man I married thought that I had lost my mind completely.

> *"Now the God of hope fill you with all joy and peace in believing, that ye may abound in hope, through the power of the Holy Ghost." Romans 15:13*

Thursday, May 15, 1997

It seemed like the longest day in the

world. I was to meet this woman for the first time face-to-face. I could not wait to get off work that day and make my way to her. I was so nervous, as I'm sure she was, but once I arrived at her home, we seemed to hit it off right from the start. In what seemed like only mere moments, we were talking and laughing like sisters, enjoying each other's company. After spending hours with this beautiful woman, I had to go home, but in my heart I didn't want to leave her. My life was changed forever that Thursday night. I thanked God as I drove home for allowing me this meeting with this woman.

"For I know the thoughts that I think toward you, saith the Lord, thoughts of peace, and not of evil, to give you an expected end." Jeremiah 29:11

In Awe of God's Plan

Once I arrived at home, I told William about my meeting with this woman. He was in awe of how well it went and said to me, "you know, this might be God's plan; it might just work out." We talked in detail about all the events that had transpired that evening, and afterwards I felt like we both had a sense of peace about us. Not long after our conversation, the phone rang and a woman's voice was on the other end of the line. Could it be? My mind and heart were racing.

"Therefore I say unto you, what things soever ye desire, when ye pray, believe that ye receive them, and ye shall have them." Mark 11:24

"You Are the Ones for My Baby"

It was around 9:45 pm. The woman I had just spent several hours talking with had called. I had the biggest lump in my throat and tears in my eyes. I prepared myself for the worst. As she spoke, her words became forever etched in my mind and heart. She said to me, "I know I haven't met your husband yet, but if he is half as nice as you, I know that you are the ones I want for this baby." I was stunned. Oh my dear sweet God, could this be true? Was I really hearing her correctly? Was she truly saying to me what I had longed to hear? Yes. Yes she was. She was a blessing and an answer to our long awaited prayers. She told us that this was and would be our baby forever! William and I just stood there in awe of the events that had just happened. We both fell to our knees weeping a waterfall of joyful tears and thanking God with all our heart and soul. God's plan, His *Divine Order*, was unfolding before our very eyes.

"And to know the love of Christ, which passeth knowledge, that ye might be filled with all the fulness of God."

"Now unto him that is able to do exceeding abundantly above all that we ask or think, according to the power that worketh in us."
Ephesians 3:19-20

CHAPTER 5

MICHAEL'S STORY: A STORY THAT CHANGED OUR LIVES FOREVER

"And the LORD God formed man of the dust of the ground, and breathed into his nostrils the breath of life; and man became a living soul."
Genesis 2:7

Tuesday, July 22, 1997

... a day that will forever be burned in our hearts and minds. The day I was truly born and the day our long-awaited son, Michael William Bridges, was born.

Sharing the Story With My Son

My son, where do I begin to tell your story of how you came to be? I don't know where to even start....but I know I never want an ending.

Son, this is your story that I feel I must share with you. It starts with daddy and me. We met in May of 1987. I was only 14 and your daddy was 20 (now don't go getting any ideas). I was very young, but your daddy swept me off my feet the first moment I met him and he still does after 21 years of marriage. I think it was love at first sight. We got married in May, 1990. We both knew we wanted to have a family from the start, but it wasn't an easy road for us. It was full of tears and anger. I wanted a baby so badly that it hurt. We waited a year after we had gotten married to begin trying to have a family. It seemed as if those years of trying just kept passing us by. With each passing month and each passing year the pain of not having a child grew and grew and became hard to bear. I felt so empty. I cried a lot, and prayed a lot. I was angry with God. I could not understand why God had not answered your daddy's and my prayers. We only wanted a baby to love and cherish.

Test after test, procedure after procedure; nothing seemed to work. I would cry out to God, and still no baby. Seven years we cried, seven years we prayed, seven years we waited. I couldn't understand why we couldn't have a beautiful baby to love and care for like everyone else around us. After seven years I finally broke. I prayed out to God like I had never prayed in my life. My prayer was "God, if you see fit to give me a child I promise I will not fail you. I will not fail this child. I will love him or her and give this child everything I can mentally, physically, spiritually and emotionally. I will not make the same mistakes I have made in the past." Michael, this prayer was all I think God wanted. God wanted me to give Him my heart and soul. For you see Michael, God did have a plan for our life and for your life. This was his *Divine Order*.

The Life-Changing Day

Mother's Day, 1997 would change my life forever, because this was the day we were told about you. Only we did not know it was "you" yet.

We were told of a woman that was five months pregnant and wanted to give her baby up for adoption. She felt you needed more than what she could give you. This was God's hand at work in all our lives; "God's *Divine Order*." I met with your birth mother that Thursday night. Right away I felt a bond with her. It was as if I had always known her. *Michael!,* she was a beautiful woman! I met with her again the next day, Friday. That night after our meeting she called the house and said to me "I know I haven't met your husband yet, but if he is as nice as you I know in my heart that you are the ones for my baby." I couldn't speak. I couldn't breathe. Could this be true? After I hung up the phone and told your dad what had just happened, he just couldn't believe it. He said to me, "this was the craziest most hare-brained idea that I had ever had; no one in her right mind would just give her baby away." I think he thought I had finally lost my mind. Our emotions were all over the place; happy, overjoyed, disbelieving, hopeful…. we had them all. Well this was again God's *Divine Order*. You see, your birth mother was not "giving you away." God had planted the seed of life for me and your dad in her. God knew from the moment you were conceived that you would be our son, our child, our baby.

Friday May 16, 1997

It was a grand day, for William and I both would go together to meet this wonderful woman and her family. We visited for the longest time. No one wanted to leave. We all had an immediate bond and from that moment on we were inseparable.

May 22, 1997

The night before we went to our first doctor's appointment (May 22, 1997) with your birth mother, my best friend Millie (who would later become your Godmother) was at the house with me. We were sitting in the floor folding little baby clothes and baby blankets talking about the new events in our life when the phone rang. My heart stopped. I thought to myself, please Lord don't let her have changed her mind, I don't think I could survive that heartache.

Let the Past Go

On the other end of the line was my foster son calling to say that he loved us and wanted to thank us for all that we had done for him because he was being adopted. After speaking with his current foster mother, she said that he and his sister were both being adopted by the same family, he just didn't know that yet. What a gift for him and his little sister. I was truly overwhelmed with joy for those beautiful children that once called us "Mom and Dad." They were truly going to have a forever home and forever Mom and Dad. By our foster son calling us that evening, your daddy and I felt it was God's *Divine Order*. That call was God's way of telling us to let the past go as He was now giving us the peace that we had so prayed for. He was telling us to close the door to our past and open the door to our future. I could feel God wrap his arms around me and hold me close to him, just like you would hold a beloved child.

God Prepared Us For You

The love between the birth parents and us grew stronger and stronger as the weeks went by and as this little baby grew and grew. Little did we know what joys God had planned for us. It was all the pain and challenges that we had gone through with foster parenting that gave us what we would need to prepare us and make us the loving parents we were about to become. Getting ready to receive God's gifts….WOW! How do you get ready for what God has been preparing for you? A birthday; a new beginning; a new chapter in our lives….the birth of our first child, our son.

Michael, God Gave You to Us

Michael, our child, our baby, through the love that God has for me and your dad, He gave you to us. Michael, you were chosen. Yes, God chose us for you and you for us. See the puzzle; see the story reveal God's love and *Divine Order* for our lives…"His" awesome plan.

My Love For You Before You Were Born

Michael, your birth mother was awesome. She wanted us to be a part of the pregnancy as much as possible. We were inseparable from the time we met her. I felt you were mine from the very beginning. I so longed to hold you, kiss you and love you. I could close my eyes and feel you growing in my heart even thought you were not in my tummy. Even though I could not feel you kick and wiggle in my tummy, you were very active in your temporary home (your birth mother's womb). She would grab my hand every time you would kick and wiggle and place it on her tummy so I could feel you move. It was such an awesome feeling. I could feel the warmth of your world as you would kick my hand. Oh, I wanted you so much. Every time you would get the hiccups I would put my ear to your warm world and hear you inside. You left me speechless.

Your birth mother was five months pregnant when we met her. We talked every day and we were together every weekend. We had fun together just hanging out, getting to know each other. She craved peanuts and Dr. Pepper while she was pregnant, so I went to the store a lot to ease her cravings. This would explain why you love peanuts and Dr. Pepper, even though you don't dump your peanuts into the Dr. Pepper.

The Ultrasound Results

We got to see you for the very first time on an ultrasound that was done at your birth mother's doctor appointment. It was that day, that moment we learned we were going to have a beautiful baby boy. What a beautiful baby. I could not wait to have you in my arms for real. It was so funny, on the day we finally got to see you for the first time, your profile actually matched your daddy's. We looked at daddy, laughing of course. Where were you five months ago, daddy? He laughed. We all laughed.

Seeing your ultrasound, we didn't know what to say. We were seeing you for the very first time. You were incredible. Your dad and I just stood there crying and in utter amazement. This was our first glimpse of you, our son. Ten fingers and ten toes and as far as we could see, you were positively perfect. Our son, could this be real? I felt as if I were in a dream, just praying I would never wake up.

Choosing Your Name

Well, as the weeks passed and we came closer and closer to really holding you, we chose your name... Michael William Bridges. You were due to arrive in this world on August 22, 1997, but you had a different plan and different date in mind. We were in the hospital four different times with your birth mother because she went into preterm labor.

July 22, 1997: Your Birth Date

On July 22, 1997, a month early, you decided it was going to be your day to come into the world and make your appearance known. At around 7:00 a.m. on the morning of July 22nd we got "the call." Your birth mother was in labor and there was no stopping it that day. We were to meet your birth mother and her husband at the hospital.

We got there at 8:00 a.m. and sat on the bench under a beautiful tree. It was a warm blue July sky. This was our day. God had planned this day just for us, this beautiful day. We were excited and nervous - all at the same time. This was the day we finally would get to have "our son" in our arms forever.

Rounding the corner of the walkway of the hospital at 8:30 a.m. were your birth mother and her husband. I felt your presence as she got closer and closer. We checked in at the hospital and we all settled into her room. Your birth mother allowed daddy and me to both stay and be a part of your delivery. How awesome to be able to be a part of your birth. It was such a long day. After laboring all day, the doctor came in and broke your birth mother's water late that afternoon hoping that would speed the process. At 10:59 p.m. Tuesday July 22, 1997 you came into our world.

Joy Overwhelming

I don't know if I even remembered to breathe at that moment. I was standing by the doctor and daddy was standing at the head of the bed. When you appeared I was speechless. All I could do was stand there as tears streamed down my face. Dad just stood, speechless. The doctor got quiet for a moment. Then finally...a cry, a long-awaited cry.

The Miracle

The doctor looked at me and said "this baby has a Guardian Angel watching over him." You see Michael, you had three true fisherman's knots in your umbilical cord. The umbilical cord was your life support system while you were in your temporary home, the womb. The knots were tight and this was cutting off your life support. The doctor said that you were a true miracle. He said he had never had a delivery that had a good outcome for the baby with knots like this. Michael... you are a miracle baby. God had this day planned and you were determined today would be "Your Birthday." God allowed you to come early because your temporary home was not safe for you any longer. It was time for your debut and you were ready to greet the world.

> *"Knowing this, that the trying of your faith worketh patience. But let patience have her perfect work, that ye may be perfect and entire, wanting nothing." James 1:3-4*

When I first saw you I could not believe my eyes. It felt as if my heart were beating out of my chest. I could not breathe. You looked so big to me and like a wadded up white sheet to your dad. I don't think he really knew what to expect or think. We were both in shock looking at the most amazing gift from God, you, our beautiful baby boy. You were not as big as I had first thought. I think the tears were clouding my eyes, because baby, you were so truly tiny. You weighed only 4lbs 15oz, but Son, you were holding your own in this world.

Your MOM Held You First

The doctor looked at me and then looked at your birth mother after you were born, most likely feeling very awkward, not knowing to whom he should hand you. I think that your birth mother picked up on his confusion and expression about the same time that I did. With a moment of silence, the doctor then asked, "who wants to hold this little fellow?" Dying to hold you, I couldn't speak. God knew my heart and without me saying a word, your birth mother spoke. She said "I think that his "MOM" would like to hold him first." Oh God, was she referring to me? I was a mom, yes that's right, I had a new name and it was "MOMMY." Tears of joy started silently streaming down my face. This was finally happening. Our family was finally starting anew.

A Gift From God

With your dad standing beside me, the nurse put you in my arms. I was shaking inside. At last, I was holding my son. O Dear God, my savior, my dearest friend, you have given me this beautiful gift, this child, to love and care for. I felt so blessed by God at that moment.

Tears of Joy

I held you for a moment and then the nurse needed to take you and do all their stuff to get you cleaned up. I didn't want to hand you over, even though I knew it would only be for just a little while. Daddy and I followed you to the hospital nursery and watched them clean you up and get you all warm. You sweet baby boy, I am so in love with you. Daddy and I just stood there in the nursery window staring at you. The tears just started streaming down my face, tears of joy, overwhelming joy. I just couldn't believe this was really happening. My dreams of having a dear sweet baby had come true.

Aunt Millie

Your Aunt Millie would be the first person, besides daddy and me to see you. She worked at the hospital and got off at 11:00 p.m. that night. She came down to be with us after work. She was and is a big part of your life. She held me and cried tears of joy along with me and your dad.

Millie, better known to you as Aunt Millie, your Godmother, has been through all our ups and downs of wanting a child. She has been a shoulder for Mommy to lean on many years. Aunt Millie sat on the floor and helped me fold your tiny little clothes the night before we even knew you were going to be a sweet little baby boy.

We Could Not Leave You

As that wonderful night started to draw to an end, Aunt Millie had to go home. That left your dad and me time to sit and soak in all the events of the day. We were not about to leave the hospital until we could leave with you to start our family of three. The hospital was so great. They let us rent a room on the third floor for only $25.00 a day. I would have paid it even if it was a $1000.00 a day because I was not about to leave you. The nursery staff was wonderful also, not only to you but to us as well. They had a little room with a rocking chair in it for our visits so we could have some private time with you. I wanted to and tried to nurse you. I know you are probably saying in your mind, "Do What!" Well, you see, I had heard about a medication that causes what is called "Induced Lactation" in a woman and I had to try it. So

I had to take medication that would hopefully make me be able to produce milk for you. I began this medication several months before you were born and then I had to stop taking it a few weeks before you arrived because it was making me sick. Needless to say, my attempt at breastfeeding you proved unsuccessful. I then was told of "Supplemental Breastfeeding," which I tried and did sometimes, but after soaking us both (a lot), the bottle was good.

CHAPTER 6

A HOMECOMING FOR MICHAEL

Friday July 25, 1997

We came home from the hospital as a family on Friday July 25, 1997. Home Sweet Home! We were now beginning our life as a family in our home, your home. You were so tiny. When you were discharged from the hospital your weight was 4lbs. 11oz. We were so in love with you. Oh, my sweet baby boy was finally home, finally ours to love and care for.

Homecoming

Our home was a very busy place that weekend. All of our family and friends could not wait to meet you. Everyone fell in love with you at first sight. Granny and Papaw, Grandmother and Granddaddy, your great grandparents, aunts, uncles and friends all came to see you. They had all waited, along with daddy and me, for 7 years to meet you. What a Homecoming you had!

Settling in as a family felt so natural, so grand. It was as if we had been practicing for this moment our whole life. God had truly blessed us with a son of our own. You were such a blessing in our lives and with each passing day we realized that this wasn't just a dream we would have to awake from, this was really real. It was our dream that had come true. The dark sad places of our past were fading away. The sun had broken through the clouds and pain of infertility and provided a true blessing from God. I would not change a thing.

The First Birthday Came Fast

Each day was sweeter than the previous one and before we knew it a whole year had passed. Where did the time go? In my mind time stood still from the moment you were in my arms. Every day brought something new to behold. It could have been as simple as you smiling at my voice, a coo, a laugh, a cry, learning to sit up on your own and many more accomplishments. Our little world as a family was in full bloom.

It was hard to believe that it was time to celebrate your One Year Birthday already. Oh how we celebrated with a Winnie the Pooh Party. I am not sure if you actually ate the cake or the cake ate you, but you had to be put in the bathtub before you could even begin to open the mountains of gifts that awaited you.

My how the days passed, so much fun, so many laughs, so many memories. Your first tooth, your first step, your first words...all the things your daddy and I thought we would never be able to see. Hearing you say "Mommy" and "Dada" just melted our hearts every time. So many blessings God has given us and your existence in our life is one of the biggest blessings of all. You are truly a blessing and a true miracle.

A Strapping Handsome Young Man

The days, months and years are still passing, but with you they are filled with joy and newness. You are now 14 years old, a strapping, handsome young man who is 5'9" and weighs 122 lbs. Quite an improvement from when you first arrived in this world. It is hard to look at you now and imagine my tiny little baby boy, but the memory of first seeing you in person is forever etched in my mind and filled with love always.

You Are a Gift From God

God has seen us through the beginning chapters of our lives and will continue to guide us through all the future chapters of our lives as a family. Our son, our child, our baby you will always be. We love you with all our hearts and thank God for you, our gift, our miracle from heaven, every day. My son, you are in our prayers always and forever will be. No matter where your life takes you, you will always have the love of God, your daddy and me.

CHAPTER 7

A SECOND TRIP DOWN INFERTILITY ROAD

"But they that wait upon the LORD shall renew their strength; they shall mount up with wings as eagles; they shall run, and not be weary; and they shall walk and not faint."
Isaiah 40:31

Days Filled With Newness and Blessings

Our days have been filled with newness and blessings as a family. Our son Michael is growing beautifully. The joys of parenting are not just a dream any longer. The dream has now become a reality. The diapers, bottles, teething and walking all seem such a blur now. Now the first day of school is upon us. Wow, where did all those years go so fast?

Thoughts of Another Baby

Well, life is good and our baby is now five years old and headed off to pre-K. It seems like just yesterday we had brought him home from the hospital. As life would have it, my maternal clock is ticking quite loud again. We're ready to have another child. Like a lot of married couples, it's time for the second baby when the first baby is around 4 or 5 years old. I think it is because once that little one starts school and becomes more independent, that longing feeling of holding your baby just kicks you right in the gut, especially when he looks at you and says "Let me do it Mommy, I am a big boy now." You realize at that moment that your baby is growing up and the years have snuck by you without you even knowing it. Maybe having that second baby will help you remember. Who knows? That's just my thought.

Well for us, we again knew conception would not be easy, but we wanted to try. We hadn't used any form of birth control in twelve years, so it was not like we were trying to prevent it from happening...it just wasn't happening. We talked about our options and decided we would drive down the infertility road once again. Who knows, maybe there will be some new routes to take this time. Besides... having one private adoption in a life-time was huge. We certainly didn't even consider that might be how our second child would come... a test of faith.

A Bumpy Road

Here's a little secret that is hard to

learn... "Don't count your chickens before they hatch." Okay, here we go. Are you buckled up? This is going to be a bumpy road ahead.

Multiple Exams Again

In 2002, when our baby boy was 5 years old, the second road of infertility began, or I should say, began again. What were we thinking? Okay God, where do we go? What route do we take? It's not that we had a GPS for this trip. Going back to the doctor, you step inside and it smells the same as it did before. The doctor looks over our records; our "Super-Duper" file of 7 years worth. Another SA and another... it looks worse than before. Now to the urologist and the physical examination. William certainly hated that exam with a passion, but he did it anyway. His physical exam was fine. The doctor said to us, "I don't know. I don't seem to find any varicoceles" (varicoceles are blockages of the grand seminal tubes). The exam seemed complete and the ultrasound showed no blockages. So what is going on?

Surgery?

We now have a referral to a Male Internal Specialist in Atlanta, Ga. Time for another road trip! Thank God for a good insurance plan because there was more and more testing. This doctor, "a Specialist, said that there were blockages, called "Bi-lateral Varicoceles." Surgery would be required to fix the problem. Our minds were racing in a thousand directions. Did we finally have an answer? Did we have the hope of conception? This was great.

William had the surgery. This wonderful man, my husband, wanted to have the surgery and give us a chance at conception. Well…. God already had plans of his own for us; His *Divine Order*. Conception would not take place this way. We again passed though a whole year and no positive pregnancy test. What next?

Attempts at IUI

We then met with my doctor and decided to try an IUI (Intrauterine Insemination) with our sperm. IUI. Oh my dear, I thought I was going to die! It was so painful. And it failed. Our hearts were broken once again. After much prayer, we decided to try another IUI, this time with a donor. We tried that twice. Each time failing and leaving us in tears. I was angry, lost and felt hopelessly alone again on this road of infertility. All the old feelings and confusions I had felt in the past attempts many years ago came flooding back. God I just don't understand. Failed surgery, three failed IUI's, pain and tears. God, is this the end of the road? You did grant us a beautiful child and for that I thank you. God please give us peace and know that this is our lot in life and help us to be happy and content with one child. The child we love and adore so very much. If one child is all you have for us, help us to find peace with one. With peace found, we will be okay, because you have blessed us in so many ways.

> *"These things I have spoken unto you, that in me ye might have peace. In the world ye shall have tribulation: but be of good cheer; I have overcome the world." John 16:33*

CHAPTER 8

A LITTLE PRAYER
ANSWERED IN A BIG WAY

"Be careful for nothing; but in every thing by prayer and supplication with thanksgiving let your requests be made known unto God."
Philippians 4:6

The Unfolding of God's *Divine Order*

Little did we know God was working on a Master Plan all along. After traveling the "Infertility Road" for 3 more years and praying for God to give us complete peace to live as a family of three, God had a different plan in mind for us. His Divine Order was about to unfold before our eyes yet again.

Our little boy was now seven years old and had started asking us for a baby brother. How do you tell your seven-year-old child that Mommy and Daddy couldn't make that happen for him? We didn't know how. Where do you even begin without confusing him even more? We told Michael to pray and if it was God's will for us to have another child and him a baby brother, God would give us that baby. Well Michael, our dear little boy, did pray for a baby brother every single night for a year (yes, I said a year) and I prayed to God every night to hear our little boy's prayers, even though in my heart I had no idea how they could be answered. God has magnified hearing when it comes to a child's prayer. His plan was in motion and we had no idea of what was in store for our family, but God did. We all need to have the faith of a child.

CHAPTER 9

FAITH OF
A MUSTARD SEED

"And Jesus said unto them, Because of your unbelief: for verily I say unto you, if ye have faith as a grain of mustard seed, ye shall say unto this mountain, Remove hence to yonder place; and it shall remove; and nothing shall be impossible unto you." Matthew 17:20

God's Timing

Faith is what we all need. No matter how great or small our prayers may be, God can answer them all perfectly, but in his own time. William and I, along with Michael, prayed for God's will. Michael was quite detailed to God with his prayer. He prayed for a baby brother.

A Second Adoption

William and I decided we would seek adoption for our second child. Why not? God had blessed us once already with a beautiful son through adoption, so why wouldn't he bless us again through adoption? We are so truly ignorant to the fact that he (Michael) is adopted. We forget that aspect of how he came to be in our lives. All we know is that he is our son; our beautiful son.

Private Adoption

I talked to my doctors and midwives and contacted many other groups and agencies just getting the word out and getting our name on any possible list available. Our first child was through a private adoption. We could have never even dreamed our second would also be a private adoption. God knew what our bank account looked like. He also knew an agency wouldn't be affordable for us. Private adoption costs only Attorney's fees and Court cost...perfect for a country middle class family.

Tuesday May 3, 2005

Tuesday May 3, 2005. What a beautiful day. I had no idea what this day would bring when I got up that morning. The morning was like all other mornings, nothing unusual or out of the ordinary routine, or at least that is what we thought. I took Michael, our now eight-year-old, to school that morning. Daddy was off that day; actually that whole week. I dropped Michael off at school telling him I loved him and hoped he had a good day just like always. Once I was back on the road headed to work, something just came over me out of nowhere,

> *"Let us therefore come boldly unto the throne of grace, that we may obtain mercy, and find grace to help in time of need." Hebrews 4:16*

The Emotional Release of Giving it All to God

I broke. I cried out to God in pain and the tears began to flow. After three long years trying to conceive a second child, I had once again come to that point of pain that I had to give it all to God. I prayed, "God, the burden is once again too heavy for me to bear. I can't carry this burden any longer. God please take this cross and this burden. Take it from me. I can't carry it any more. It is too heavy. You must carry it for me. God, I am too weak. Please take this burden from me. It is yours. Give me strength and peace."

> *"But thou, when thou prayest, enter into thy closet, and when thou hast shut thy door, pray to thy Father which is in secret; and thy Father which seeth in secret shall reward thee openly." Matthew 6:6*

A Phone Call

I wiped my tears and got to work. I don't know how I even got there because I had been crying so hard and praying so deeply. When I got to work, my boss, Dolly, told me that my friend Scarlett had called and wanted me to call her back. Jokingly Dolly said, "Maybe she is calling about a baby." Well, little did she know and little did I know that my friend **was** calling about a baby!

A baby, yes, a baby. I did not believe what I had just heard. It had only been one hour since I had poured my heart out to God with my pain and burden. God and His *Divine Order*. It's shocking sometimes.

Do You Want This Baby?

I called my friend Scarlett, and yes, she had been told of a single, beautiful, El Salvador woman who wanted to give her newborn up for adoption. Out of her mouth came the question I was not expecting to hear. "Do you want this baby?" My heart stopped and there was complete silence. Oh my dear, precious God, was this true? Was this happening? I, without question, knew in my heart that this was God's plan. This truly had put a new meaning to the phrase "What are friends for?" I was in total shock! Some may call this phone call a coincidence. NO WAY! I call this "God's *Divine Order*." God had put three of my dear friends in the right place at the right time. His time and his place.

God Uses Friends

He put my friends Perry, Jackie and Scarlett in the exact path and presence of this woman to carry out his plan. God does have his people here on earth to act as angels to allow his plans to be put in action. Thank God for these dear friends and for these dear friends to allow themselves to act as God's helpers. They will always have a special spot in my heart.

Shocked

God had been working on this plan for quite some time, we just didn't know it. Can you spell "Shocked"? I mean, hello, we had only gotten the word out two weeks before and I had only just dumped my burdens on God one hour before the phone call. God works faster than our brains can comprehend and a whole lot faster than when we try to do things ourselves. I now knew why I had not conceived in those previous months. It was because you can't conceive if you already have, and my child had already been conceived.

Divine Order: Tuesday May 3, 2005

Okay, back to the phone call. The question was "Do you want a beautiful baby boy?" His birth mother is from El Salvador, his birth father is from Columbia. That didn't matter to me. This baby could have been from Mars and I would have still taken him. This was God's plan, His *Divine Order*. My reply was "Yes, Yes, Yes. I do need to call William though." I called the house and got no answer. William was off that week and was outside working and did not have his cell phone with him. I was in a panic. I had to reach him ASAP. I called my mother and explained to her that I needed to get in touch with William. She drove to my house and ordered him to call me right away. He called me right back. I know that I was talking in circles, I had to be. I told him the story and he was in shock also. God does have a funny way of doing that sometimes. William so did not care that this baby was of another nationality. His only statement and question to me was "Call the bank, and how fast do you think our attorney can get all this together?"

Well, I didn't even have any worries about those things, because I knew if God had this all planned, he had that stuff planned too. So William and I were "Yes, Yes, Yes" to this baby. I called Scarlett and she said she would speak to the birth mother about us. The birth mother was happy with Scarlett for finding us for her baby. She said "We were what she had prayed for."

"And we know that all things work together for good to them that love God, to them who are the called according to his purpose."
Romans 8:28

CHAPTER 10

BRETT'S STORY

Brett Logan Bridges, born May 3, 2005, 7lbs.13oz

"Be still, and know that I am God."
Psalm 46:10

My dear sweet baby Brett; my miracle. You are so beautiful. From the moment I was told of you, I knew that you were meant to be my son. You were born on Tuesday May 3, 2005 weighing 7lb 13oz. What a special day that was. We did not get to meet you until Thursday May 5, 2005 but in my heart I already knew you were born to be our son. The time between your birth and when we finally got to meet you were the longest two days of our lives. I cried for those two days, longing to hold you in my arms and kiss your sweet face. It was killing me knowing that I had to wait those two days to see you, hold you and bring you home with us, my baby, my son.

What a Day That Will Be

Well, Thursday May 5th finally came

and what a day it was! Not only would we get to see you and bring you home, it was also mine and your Daddy's 15th wedding anniversary. How 'bout that, you came home on our anniversary – cool don't ya think? What an amazing way to celebrate an anniversary!

Okay, two days to get ready for you and I had nothing. For you see, your big brother Michael was eight years old and we did not have any baby stuff around the house. Everybody was so great to us. Diapers and all kinds of baby stuff showed up on our front door just for you. What a blessing that was.

Meeting Brett the First Time

Okay, meeting you for the first time, I am losing my breath just thinking about it. You were at the hospital and we arrived a around 9 am., so anxious to see you. We waited and waited for our attorney to meet us there. Finally around 9:45a.m., after waiting for what seemed like an eternity, he arrived. We were now only moments away from having you in our arms. Daddy, the attorney and I took the elevator to the second floor of the hospital. My heart was pounding the whole way. We got off the elevator at the mother/baby unit and let the case manager know we were there. We all sat down to wait for the case manager to come. That was the longest 30 minutes, it felt more like 30 days!

"Ask, and it shall be given you; seek, and ye shall find; knock, and it shall be opened unto you: For everyone that asketh receiveth; and he that seeketh findeth; and to him that knocketh it shall be opened."
Matthew 7:7-8

The Case Manager

The case manager finally came and asked if we had planned to meet your birth mother face-to-face. Of course we wanted to meet her and our prayer was that she wanted to meet us also. Case management went to her room with an interpreter and within just a few moments it was time for us to finally meet her. My heart was pounding and my hands were shaking. I had a million things going through my head as we arrived at her door. As we opened the door to her room it was like opening the door to heaven. To our surprise, you were there with her. Dad and I felt drawn to her immediately. You were wrapped tightly in a little blue and pink stripped hospital blanket. All we could see was your sweet little head poking out of the blanket that cradled you in a little nursery bed. You had a head full of black hair.

Meeting Your Birth Mother

Dad went over to your birth mother first. He leaned down to this beautiful young woman who was sitting on the side of the bed next to you. She had long black hair just like you, beautiful cream-colored skin and big beautiful dark brown eyes that were so kind and gentle. She wrapped her arms around your dad and hugged him with such love and what seemed to be gratitude. Daddy then stepped aside and I leaned toward her also to give her a hug. She pulled me down beside her and hugged me with the same love and gratitude as she had shown your dad. We hugged and cried for the longest time. Here we were, two women with unconditional love for this one little boy who was, to both of us, our son. Both with an uncontested love for this baby, I would be bringing you home and she would be letting you go. Both Moms doing what God had planned. I was bringing you home forever and she, loving you forever by letting you go.

We sat and held hands, smiling and crying together. With the help of an interpreter we talked for awhile, telling your birth mother a little about us and our family. Tears fell from both of our faces like a cascading waterfall. My heart felt as if it had stopped when this beautiful woman asked if we would like to hold you. She stood at your bedside and picked you up with such gentleness and placed you in my arms.

The tears flowed down both of our faces as I held you. Your birth mother reached out to my face and gently wiped my tears. She wiped my tears, not hers. This was truly a moment of no words. God's love and beauty were shining through this woman, for her touch spoke a thousand words to my very soul. She then backed away for a moment to give daddy and me some space and time with just you, our son, our beautiful new baby boy.

Holding Brett the First Time

Daddy and I held you and looked you over from one end to the other, just in awe of your beauty. Ten little fingers, ten little toes, and a head full of hair. This perfect little being was our son. As time was coming together and we were re-entering the reality world, we had to do all the legal paperwork and stuff to officially make you ours. After a lot of "yes's and no's" and signatures had been taken care of, our attorney asked your birth mother if she had anything she wanted to add or say to us. Her words were like the softness of a cool spring morning with the sounds of birds singing and the warmth of the first morning sun on your face after a long cold winter.

A Birth Mother's Request

She said she wanted us to love you and give you everything that she could not and to keep God in your house. In her culture to keep God in your house meant to keep God in your heart and life always. We promised her we would do just that. After the legal paperwork had been completed, it was time for the final most important thing to be done. It was time to get you ready to go home. Go home with us, Mommy and Daddy, to your big brother and new family that were waiting anxiously at home for your arrival. All of whom loved you even before they knew you.

Communicating With Sign Language

Daddy went to get your car seat so we could take you home. Case management and the interpreter left also so all that was left in this still, soft room was your birth mother, me and our attorney, who was sitting in the corner giving us our final time together as mothers.

Your birth mother and I sat on the bed, just the two of us with you. Even with words not understood through our language barrier, it was amazing how God gave us our own language with each other through our touch, smiles and tears. We did have some broken words of understanding, but mainly communicated with the language of emotions. Hand gestures and body movements can say a lot between two people.

Your Homegoing Outfit

Your birth mother had an outfit that she wanted you to wear home, even though it was two sizes too big for you. I was so honored for you to wear it home. She dressed you and got you ready to give to me. She also had a big, beautiful, soft blanket that she wanted you to have. It had a big soft yellow duck/chicken coming out of a shell on it. After she got you ready, she sat on her bed and held you for a moment. I asked her if I could take a picture of you and her. She laughed and was worried about her hair and not having any makeup on. We both laughed. She was beautiful without any makeup. I took a picture for you of you and her together. Our time with her was precious and profound.

Final Good-bye to the Birth Mother

Dad came back a little while later, after getting the car seat ready for you. The time had come for us to say our final good-bye and take you home to start our family. What once was a home with just daddy and me, was now a home filled with two beautiful sons who were our most precious gifts from God and truly his *Divine Order* for our lives. Two gifts of life, love in abundance and a family of four forever.

This *Divine Order.*

"In every thing give thanks: for this is the will of God in Christ Jesus concerning you."
I Thessalonians 5:18

CHAPTER 11

ALIEN INVASION

The Awesome Road

The road has truly been awesome. What a long strange trip it's been. I say that very light-heartedly.

Where have all the years gone? I think about where God has brought us from, this wonderful Journey, this wonderful Plan, this wonderful Road God has prepared for us, not to travel alone but to travel with him, with our family and friends. How awesome.

I can't help but think about the times I worried about having babies and God granted me that. About worrying when they were sick or hurt and God took care of that. About when I had to go to work after my first-born and the worry of having to put him in daycare. God took care of that, and boy, did he take care of that. He sent Angels along the way to take care of my baby while I was at work. He certainly took care of that when Michael was about 2 years old. He sent an Angel who became "Nana Patsy."

Divine Order and Nana Patsy

She kept Michael from the time he was 2 years old until he started to school, then 8 years later when Brett was born, she only had one spot left in her small private daycare. When Brett was born, I called "Nana Patsy" and you could have heard her from across town laughing as she said "you know I only have one spot left and I had a call 2 weeks ago from someone asking me if I had a spot, and something just kept telling me to say that I was full, so I didn't fill the spot. Now I know why." God had that spot reserved for Brett, so yes, God took care of that also. Nana Patsy had Brett from the time he was 13 weeks old (when I had to go back to work) until the time he started school. God is good and he does send us Angels here on earth.

I ask you, the reader, to pray when it's time for you to go back to work that God would send you a "Nana Patsy" as an Angel on earth. She truly wasn't just a sitter as she had such an impact on my children and our life and our family that she is family to us.

Teen Spirit

As days pass and time flies, the children grow and grow, no longer fitting in Aunt Concon's sock drawer. You once couldn't get enough of Snuggle Fabric Softener and the smell of Dreft, Johnson & Johnson Baby Lotion and the smell of that freshly bathed lavender-smelling baby; but as time passes their new smells fill the house. The smell of dirty little boys and teen spirit. Yes, I said it. "TEEN SPIRIT!" Oh my, that will forever be etched in my mind, not to mention my nose!!!!

Children Become Alien

They do become mad scientists and set off firecrackers in the house! Thank God we didn't come home to find a pile of ashes made from the house that we once called home. His thinking was that a whole new bottle of Febreze will cover up the smell of smoke. NOT!!!

Do know that Sunblock 50 is for the pool and not the kitchen counter. (Way too many TV commercials about a clean counter and salsa bowls sliding faster!!)

Hedge trimmers are made for OUTSIDE! Broken bones do heal; just stay away from Monkey Bars and showing off in front of girls, sliding down bleachers on the football field.... And this is only Michael!!!!

We haven't even gotten to this place of *Alien Invasion* with Brett. We know that the time will come; we just pray we live through it with Michael first! God being our helper and lots of prayer and patience, a good house and Medical Insurance!!!!

The Instruction Book for Kids

They say that kids don't come with instruction books, but I am finding they do. The greatest book of all – The Holy Bible – God's little instruction book for us all.

CHAPTER 12

A RESTING PLACE

"Come unto me, all ye that labour and are heavy laden, and I will give you rest.

Take my yoke upon you, and learn of me; for I am meek and lowly in heart: and ye shall find rest unto your souls.

For my yoke is easy, and my burden is light." Matthew 11:28-30

The Roads We Traveled

We so hope you have enjoyed reading our stories which are really addressed to our boys. To us life is good. To us their stories have so much to tell. As you have seen in these stories, love, hope and faith unfold each step of the way. Emotions ran deep while writing their stories. As each of their stories share a lot of similarities, they are also unique and priceless, just as our boys are unique and priceless.

It has been a long road traveled to get where we are today. First with the road of infertility and then with the road of adoption, with many curves and many challenges, but we made it through with God's direction. Our first adoption went smoothly. A total of four months, start to finish. Finalizing the day before Thanksgiving 1997, Michael was four months old. Our second adoption had some bumps, nothing major, just a lot of red tape and paperwork mishaps that had to be corrected. It took a total of two years for this adoption to finalize in May of 2007 when Brett was two years old. Thank God everything was finished.

Pain to Make Us Grow

We would not change anything from start to finish with either of our boys. It takes rain to make the flowers grow, just as it takes pain to make us grow. The love we have for our boys runs rich and deep and can never be broken. Often people have said to me, "Oh, you're so lucky you didn't have to go through all the labor pain" and I just think to myself, "Whatever... if you only knew." I did go through labor. No, it was not the "normal" labor when having a child. It was much harder and filled with much heartache. Seven years of infertility before I was blessed with my first child and then another three years before I was blessed with my second child. Grant you, my pain was not a vaginal labor pain, but a real and physical pain in my heart that is indescribable unless you have been through it yourself. So believe me, I did go through labor pains, the only difference is that mine was a labor of love and faith for nineteen years.

CHAPTER 13

FINAL THOUGHTS

This Story is Our Story

This story is our story; God's *Divine Order* for our lives. To whomever reads our story, please know that this is not just about infertility and adoption. Our story is also about something we hope you have already found out for yourself. It is about Faith, Hope, Love and Trust that God truly does have a plan for you and your life. Whether it is wanting a family, dealing with divorce, or grieving the loss of a loved one, God does love you and has a plan for you. From the day that you are born, God has a plan for your life and a direction for you to go. As humans, we may not understand why God puts us through certain situations of life, but as Christians we must have faith in His plan. As the old saying goes "That which does not kill us will make us stronger." God knows just how far the willow tree will bend and what it takes to make it stronger.

God has a *Divine Order* for each and every one of us. Please know that whatever your pain is we are praying that you seek and find your way through Jesus Christ our Lord and Savior.

BLESSINGS ALWAYS,

> *"I can do all things through Christ which strengtheneth me."* Philippians 4:13

Where Do I Go Now?

I guess you could ask the question, "where did you go from here?"

I ask you, "where are you going from here?" I'm not judging you.

I'm judging myself. These writings are a glimpse into my life and the stories of my boys are the blessings that unfolded in my life. They are true examples of God's Love and Great Works; "Miracles" in my life. How did we come to know these were not just things that happened to us? Were they things or coincidence? Well that is a very deep and profound question. The question really being WHAT or WHO brought us to this place of knowing God is real. God is good. God is powerful yet a Loving God.

He is with us every minute of every day. When did we come to understand God and know He and only He is the air we breathe?

The Creator of Life.

The Creator of ALL and I do mean ALL. Jesus said in John 14:6 *"I am the way, the truth, and the life: no man cometh unto the Father, but by me."*

He is THE ONLY WAY.

I can do nothing on my own. I can not create life. I can not calm the storm and that includes the storms in my life. Some have said, what doesn't kill you will make you stronger. True, if we know WHO is truly in control of our life and our destiny.

He has a plan; a *"Divine Order."* Who being God. He is our source. I can do nothing, but with God I can do anything within His will. With God all things are possible. (Mark 10:27)

We are given free will. We are given choices. Choices to do right and wrong. As a child of God, He put's that still small voice in us to know right from wrong. The choice is ours for the taking.

The Amazing God

You may be saying OK GIRL, I have had enough of you. Well enough of me I can understand, but enough of God, no, I can not understand. He is the most AMAZING,

AWESOME God. The COOLEST!

Am I a Bible scholar? No, not at all. I only know what I read and the teachings of God's word. I only know what God gives me in my mind, body and soul. I asked God to come into my heart, mind, body and soul. That is where He lives in me. He lives in me because I invited Him in when He came knocking on my heart.

> *"Behold, I stand at the door, and knock: if any man hear my voice, and open the door, I will come in to him."* Rev 3:20

The Most Amazing, Profound Word to Me

The most AMAZING, PROFOUND word to me is FAITH.

Faith in knowing what you can not see, but knowing it is real.

God is Real!

My dear friend Billy asked me one time, "How did you and William come to this place of understanding of God and knowing He is real?" My answer to Billy was, "Well, I don't really know. It is a daily progression. It is daily prayer and desire to understand our Creator and to know that we did not create our own substance. Someone much greater did that, and that someone being Jesus Christ our Lord and Savior. He is our past, present and future."

Matthew 7:7 tells us:

"Seek and ye shall find."

Jesus is sufficient in every aspect of our life.

Surrender it ALL to God. The big stuff and the small stuff.

You will never be sorry. I promise you this.

"For by grace are ye saved through faith...it is the gift of God."
Ephesians 2:8

Footprints

One night a man had a dream. He dreamed he was walking along the beach with the LORD. Across the sky flashed scenes from his life. For each scene, he noticed two sets of footprints in the sand; one belonged to him, and the other to the LORD.

When the last scene of his life flashed before him, he looked back at the footprints in the sand. He noticed that many times along the path of his life there was only one set of footprints. He also noticed that it happened at the very lowest and saddest times of his life.

This really bothered him and he questioned the LORD about it. "LORD, you said that once I decided to follow you, you'd walk with me all the way. But I have noticed that during the most troublesome times in my life, there was only one set of footprints. I don't understand why when I needed you the most you would leave me."

The LORD replied, "My precious, precious child, I love you and would never leave you. During your times of trial and suffering, when you see only one set of footprints, it was then that I carried you."

Mary Stevenson

The Lord's Prayer

Our Father which art in heaven, Hallowed be thy name.

Thy kingdom come. Thy will be done in earth, as it is in heaven.

Give us this day our daily bread. And forgive us our debts, as we forgive our debtors.

And lead us not into temptation, but deliver us from evil: For thine is the kingdom, and the power, and the glory, for ever. Amen

Matthew 6:9-13

"Not Flesh Of My Flesh"

"Not flesh of my flesh, Nor bone of my bone, But still miraculously my own, Never forgot for a single minute, You didn't grow under my heart — but in it."

Author: Fleur Conkling Heylinger

ABOUT THE AUTHOR

April Dawn Bridges is a proud, hard-working, dedicated mother and adoring wife whose faith and trust in God is evident in her daily life. April Dawn is just an ordinary country girl, who with her husband, William, are the proud parents of two beautiful boys which inspired her to write this book.

They have suffered through the hardships of infertility and been blessed by adoption. "And she is totally ignorant to the fact that her kids are adopted." To her they are true gifts from God. It is her hope that this book will help others who must suffer the burden of infertility and that they will find there is hope in the beauty of adoption.

She has truly cried each and every tear and has felt pain that could never be faked. In her book she offers all her experiences as a guide to your own happy beginning. Her prayer is that you too see God's *Divine Order* in your own life.

[Publisher's note: April Bridges is willing to answer any questions that you may have. Please send an email to: aprildawnbridges@yahoo.com]

ABOUT THIS BOOK

Infertility and Adoption: A Story of Divine Order is the account of one couple's trials and blessings. April Dawn shares her family's story in an honest and divinely inspired wish for other families to find their own blessings as they have. It is truly a touching story of Hope, Love and Faith.

You will see how her faith in God kept her on her true path to Motherhood. With all the twists, turns and dead ends she faced, it was God's love and shining light that kept her steady in the dark times of her journey to motherhood.

Psalm 23

The Lord is my shepherd; I shall not want.

He maketh me to lie down in green pastures: he leadeth me beside the still waters.

He restoreth my soul: he leadeth me in the paths of righteousness for his name's sake.

Yea, though I walk through the valley of the shadow of death, I will fear no evil: for thou art with me; thy rod and thy staff they comfort me.

Thou preparest a table before me in the presence of mine enemies: thou anointest my head with oil; my cup runneth over.

Surely goodness and mercy shall follow me all the days of my life: and I will dwell in the house of the Lord for ever.

APPENDIX

HOW TO KNOW GOD

God is not hard to get to know. He loves you and love is one of His characteristics. **1 John 4:16** says: *And we have known and believed the love that God hath to us. God is love.* He has demonstrated His love in so many ways that it is hard to decide where to start, except to start where He wants every person to start. Where is that?

> *I. John 10:10 I am come that they might have life, and that they might have it more abundantly.*

These are the Words of Jesus Christ. Also, He said, "**I am He**" in John 8:24. What He is saying is that He is God. He gave us innumerable proofs that He is God while He was here. He wanted us to "have life," and to "have it more abundantly." Throughout history there have been millions who have testified: He has given me "life more abundantly." You can have 'life more abundantly' too. God is love and He wants you to know how!

> *II. Romans 3:23 For all have sinned, and come short of the glory of God.*

Sin is missing the mark. The mark is the standard God has set. The standard is reflected in the Ten Commandments. If you miss any one of those standards, you have sinned.

1. *Exodus 20:3* Thou shalt have no other gods before me.

2. *Exodus 20:4* Thou shalt not make unto thee any graven image, or any likeness of any thing that is in heaven above, or that is in the earth beneath, or that is in the water under the earth:

3. *Exodus 20:7* Thou shalt not take the name of the LORD thy God in vain; for the LORD will not hold him guiltless that taketh his name in vain.

4. *Exodus 20:8* Remember the sabbath day, to keep it holy.

5. *Exodus 20:12* Honour thy father and thy mother: that thy days may be long upon the land which the LORD thy God giveth thee.

6. *Exodus 20:13* Thou shalt not kill.

7. *Exodus 20:14* Thou shalt not commit adultery.

8. *Exodus 20:15* Thou shalt not steal.

9. *Exodus 20:16* Thou shalt not

bear false witness against thy neighbour.

10. *Exodus 20:17 Thou shalt not covet thy neighbour's house, thou shalt not covet thy neighbour's wife, nor his manservant, nor his maidservant, nor his ox, nor his ass, nor any thing that is thy neighbour's.*

God says that **all** have sinned. (Romans 3:23) He says it this way also; "All we like sheep have gone astray; we have turned every one to his own way." (Isaiah 53:6) Although we don't understand completely, we do know that when we sin it causes turmoil in our life and in this world. The Bible says it this way: "For we know that the whole creation groaneth and travaileth in pain." (Rom 8:22)

Since God loves us, He wants us to be free of this "pain." He also wants to be where we are because He loves us. He cannot be where sin is found because he is pure and holy. It is like mixing yeast, a symbol for sin, into bread. The yeast spreads throughout the bread like an infection. Therefore, we must be and are separated from God who is sinless and holy. The Bible says it like this:

"For the wages of sin *is* death." (Romans 6:23) The infection of sin leads to death. You cannot cure the infection by philosophy, religion, or good works. These are man's efforts to achieve "abundant" life and they don't work. The scourge of sin is so terrible that something only God could do will remove it.

> *III.   But, "God commendeth his love toward us, in that, while we were yet sinners, Christ died for us." (Romans 5:8)*

Sin is such a horrible curse in and on this world that the shedding of blood was necessary to save us from the infection. God loves us so "that He gave His only begotten Son, that whosoever believeth in Him should not perish but have everlasting life." (Jn. 3:16) Remember, the penalty for sin is death. Just as the price for breaking the law has to be paid by a fine or prison time, a price has to be paid for sin.

I once heard a story that makes this point clear. A Roman General was sitting in judgment of "law breakers" when a very elderly man, about 90 years of age, came before the General for adjudication or assigning the penalty. The penalty for the old man's crime was set by law and could not be changed. The penalty was 39 lashes with a whip. The penalty could not be cancelled according to Roman law. The General knew the lashing would kill the old man, so he stripped off his clothes and substituted for the old man. This is a true story. The following information is true also. A perfect, sinless substitute is required by God to fulfill the penalty of death because of sin. God was willing to give us His perfect, sinless Son, Jesus Christ, to fulfill the requirement of death. Just as amazing was the willingness of Jesus Christ to die for you and me on the Cross. *John 15:13 Greater love hath no man than this, that a man lay down his life for his friends.*

> *IV.   But God commendeth his love toward us, in that, while we were yet sinners, Christ died for us. (Romans 5:8)*

Notice that the Scripture says: "while we were yet sinners" that "Christ died for us." Just like the old man who was still a debtor to the Roman law, the General paid the price for his "sin." Our General, the Lord Jesus Christ, asks us to appreciate the gift of eternal life and to turn from our sins. Can't you just imagine that the Roman General told the elderly man never to break the law again.

> *V.   And   the   times   of   this ignorance God winked at; but now commandeth all men every where to repent. [Acts 17:30]*

One must turn from sin (breaking the law) to God, which is repentance. This must be a sincere "turning" in the heart from rebellion to becoming obedient "in the heart" to God. Jesus pointed the way to God.

> **VI.** *Jesus saith unto him, I am the way, the truth, and the life: no man cometh unto the Father, but by me.* (John 14:6)

Jesus, who is God, set the rules. He paid the price. He pointed the way by the Cross. But He also set the rule that "no man cometh unto the Father, but by me." (Jn. 14:6) You must believe who the Lord Jesus Christ is, the work that He did on the Cross for you, and turn from "your wicked ways." You will not know everything immediately, and God does not require you to know everything before He saves you. He must see that you have a sincere heart, and are willing to set out on a journey with Him as He teaches you.

> **VII.** *For I delivered unto you first of all that which I also received, how that Christ died for our sins according to the scriptures; 4And that he was buried, and that he rose again the third day according to the scriptures: 5And that he was seen of Cephas, then of the twelve: 6After that, he was seen of above five hundred brethren at once; of whom the greater part remain unto this present, but some are fallen asleep.* (1Corinthians 15:3-6)

Jesus said, *"I am He,"* and proved to us that He is God by His resurrection. He proved

He loved us by dying for us to pay the penalty of *our* sin. He was our substitute.

VIII. *But as many as received him, to them gave he power to become the sons of God, even to them that believe on his name: (John 1:12)*

We cannot know all the ramifications of sin because we cannot see "everything," just as we cannot see the wind, or sound waves, or sin. We see the results of sin, but not sin. Similarly, we cannot know all there is to know about God or we would be God. This much we do know. Death in the Words of God is described as separation from God, and results, after dying, in eternal separation from God in a place called Hell. He is willing to save you from the penalty of death by simply receiving Him by faith. You do not have to know everything. There will be a day when everything will be explained, but for now God says "believe on His name," the name of Jesus Christ, and He will give you eternal life. John 3:15 says very clearly: "*That whosoever believeth in him should not perish, but have eternal life.* He repeated this statement in the very next verse to be certain we understand. Eternal life is being present with God where there will be no tears, sadness, sickness, hunger, or pain. You are saved from eternal torment.

IX. *For by grace are ye saved through faith; and that not of*

yourselves: it is the gift of God: Not
of works, lest any man should boast.
(Ephesians 2:8-9)

There is no philosophy, religion, work, or good living that will save you. You simply have to ask God to save you from the penalty of sin because you believe that Jesus Christ is the Son of God, that He died for you, and that He rose from the dead. He loves you and wants to give you this free gift for simply saying and believing in your heart, "that Jesus died for **me**."

John 5:24 Verily, verily, I say unto
you, He that heareth my words, and
believeth on him that sent me, hath
everlasting life, and shall not come
into condemnation; but is passed
from death unto life.

It doesn't get any clearer than John 5:24. If you believe Him, simply tell God you do. You will be saved. THAT'S IT! There is not one other thing you have to do. You should also tell someone about your decision.

That if thou shalt confess with thy
mouth the Lord Jesus, and shalt
believe in thine heart that God hath
raised him from the dead, thou shalt
be saved. (Romans 10:9)

When you are saved, God changes you. You will sense the change. The change allows

God to see Christ in you. The change also allows God to live in you. Know ye not that ye are the temple of God, and *that* the Spirit of God dwelleth in you? (1Corinthians 3:16)

If you asked God to save you, welcome to the kingdom of God. Join a body of Bible believing saints [a church] and worship the Creator with them.